Take Charge of

YOUR Future:

A 1-2-3 GUIDE TO MAKING GOOD CAREER CHOICES

RODERICK S. BAKER

Take Charge of Your Future:
A 1-2-3 Guide to Making Good Career Choices

ISBN: 1482043386
ISBN-13: 978-1482043389

Library of Congress Control Number: 2013901191
CreateSpace Independent Publishing Platform, North Charleston, SC

Interior photo credits: Roderick S. Baker
Unless noted otherwise
Author photo: James A. Bowey
Cover design: Dave Piro of Piro Design

http://www.takechargeseries.com

Dedicated to all college and university students who want to make good career choices!

This guidebook is adapted from the keynote speech delivered for the Shadow Program at the Rotary Club of Winona, Minnesota, November 19, 2008.

*Your purchase makes a difference!
A portion of each sale of this guidebook will be donated to The Rotary Foundation of Rotary International which helps fund development projects and peace-building activities around the world.*

Table *of* Contents

Acknowledgements:

Thank you to all the students and teachers with whom I have come into contact over the years. You are the inspiration for this guidebook! A special thank you to Amber Shoutz, who helped make this guidebook a reality. I am also grateful for input from Charlene Baumbich, Betty Nelson, Ivy Miller, Terri Markos, Janet Seidman, Jane Walczak, Nancy Hewison, Jane Hamblin, Ian Yesilonis, Charles Watkinson, Sarah Huerta, Chris Evans, James A. Bowey, Dave Piro, my project team at CreateSpace, and my parents. Finally, to Moira Corcoran, thank you for your encouragement!

Introduction

Has someone ever asked you "What do you want to be when you grow up?" or "What are you going to do after graduation?" Whether you are a first-year college student or ready to graduate, finding answers to these questions can be daunting.

The purpose of *Take Charge of Your Future: A 1-2-3 Guide to Making Good Career Choices* is to help you find answers to the questions above by guiding you through the following three steps:

- ➢ Where am I?
- ➢ Where do I want to go?
- ➢ How am I going to get there?

You may not know exactly where you are going to be a year from now, but that's OK.

Take Charge of Your Future: A 1-2-3 Guide to Making Good Career Choices weaves together a brief collection of thoughts, stories, and quotations that I hope can provide you with tools you can use now and for years to come.

My father often refers to these three steps as the triangle for decision making. It's worth repeating them:

- ➤ Where am I?
- ➤ Where do I want to go?
- ➤ How am I going to get there?

Let's develop each of these steps and examine them individually in the context of making good career choices.

Step 1: Where Am I?

Know thyself.
—*Oracle of Delphi*

Each of us is unique! (Photo of Ahu Tongariki, Easter Island)

In February 1994, I was training for the Peace Corps in Cochabamba, Bolivia. I had been in the country for about two weeks and had just started living with a native family. It was evening, and I was eating dinner at a small table in my bedroom in their adobe-brick home. I started thinking to myself, "Oh my gosh, I'm in Bolivia—for two years! When I'm a volunteer, I'm going to have to teach Bolivians about agriculture, and I can't even identify a potato plant! Not only that, but I'm going to have to teach them about agriculture in Spanish!"

I really started getting worked up. Fortunately, and this is where the adage "Know thyself" came into play, I know that I can write myself out of a bad mood or an anxious situation in fewer than thirty minutes. I pulled out my journal and started writing. I clearly remember writing: "Take one day at a time, Rod. What do I have to do tonight? All I can do is finish this supper in front of me, do my Spanish homework, and then go to bed. The Peace Corps has three months of training for a reason: they know we will be relatively prepared to go into our villages by the end of the three months. If we don't know the answer to a question, we will at least know what questions to ask to figure it out." I started to relax. That was the moment when I really learned how valuable it is to take one day at a time.

Self-Discovery

To help answer the question "Where Am I?" a little self-exploration is necessary.

Ask yourself the following questions:

> ➢ Where am I at this point in my life?
> ➢ What have I done?
> ➢ Who am I?

Make a self-assessment or a self-inventory.

> ➢ What do I like to do?
> ➢ What turns me off?
> ➢ What skills do I have?
> ➢ How do I share with others?
> ➢ How do I contribute to my family, school, and community?

Write the answers to these or similar questions on the next page or in a journal. These answers will help you define who you are and where you are right now.

Worksheet for Self-Assessment

What do I like to do?

_____

_____

_____

What turns me off?

_____

_____

_____

What skills do I have?

_____

_____

_____

How do I share with others?

_____

_____

_____

How do I contribute to my family, school, and community?

_____

_____

_____

From _Take Charge of Your Future: A 1-2-3 Guide to Making Good Career Choices_ by Roderick S. Baker © 2013

Where am I? Discovering the beauty of Glacier Grey in southern Chile's Torres del Paine National Park with Peace Corps buddy Glenn Cerosaletti on the left.

Photo: Ian Yesilonis

How Do I Know More about Myself?

Have you taken the Myers-Briggs Type Indicator® (MBTI) personality inventory[1] or a similar personal inventory? If you have not, seek out that test. Keep the results. The MBTI places you into one of sixteen different personality types. It can help you understand how you best recharge or re-energize yourself by either being around people or having quiet time to yourself. You discover ways in which you best deal with others and handle situations. You can learn a lot about yourself through these types of personal inventory tests.

One of the important sayings of the Oracle of Delphi of ancient Greece was "Know thyself." The more you know about yourself, the better equipped you will be for your next step.

Being Honest

It's important to be honest with yourself. This helps you stay in touch with reality.

---

1   Check out http://www.myersbriggs.org.

As Shakespeare's Lord Polonius said:

This above all: To thine own self be true,
And it must follow, as the night the day.
Thou canst not then be false to any man.
— *Hamlet, I.3.78-80*

When you are true to yourself, your friends will look up to you and the integrity that you evoke. On the flip side, you can sense when someone is being phony. You are less likely to trust what that person is saying if you feel he or she is dishonest. You even know when you aren't being true to yourself.

Being honest and true to yourself helps you set realistic goals. Having realistic goals is an important aspect of making good career choices.

Your answer to the question "Where am I?" gives you a starting point for your next steps. As you understand where you are, who you are, what makes you tick, what you like, and what you don't like, you will gain a better foundation for the second step...

Step 2: Where Do I Want to Go?

Shoot for the moon. Even if you miss it, you will land among the stars.
—Les Brown

In April 2000 I was fortunate to be headed back to Bolivia for a month on a Group Study Exchange team through Rotary International,[2] a public service organization. During the trip, one of my teammates, Andrea, had said to me, "Rod, a year from now I want to be teaching English in Vietnam." I thought to myself, "Wow—now that's some goal!" My friend Andrea had a very clear vision of what she wanted her next step to be. When you ask yourself where you want to go, you're answering it with a goal.

President John F. Kennedy's goal in May of 1961 of sending an American to the moon and back safely by the end of the decade was a clear and well-defined goal. The

---

2   Check out http://www.rotaryinternational.org.

country could visualize it. NASA had a clear mission. It would take the completion of many smaller goals to make JFK's goal a reality, but people knew what they were working toward.

SMART Goals

When you set a goal, make it a SMART Goal. SMART is an acronym for specific, measurable, attainable, results-oriented, and time-framed.

> ➤ Specific—clearly state what you want.
> ➤ Measurable—decide what you will use to assess your progress toward achieving your goal. Include smaller steps to help you reach your goal.
> ➤ Attainable—know that you have the ability to reach your goal even if others haven't.
> ➤ Results-oriented—clearly define the outcome you want.
> ➤ Time-framed—state your completion date.

There are different variations of the SMART acronym. Others include R for realistic or relevant and T for time-bound or trackable. The version here using specific, measurable, attainable, results-oriented, and time-framed was first introduced to me where I work at RiverSide Electronics. They were presented in the text *Developing Performance Goals and Standards* by the Vital Learning Corporation. I really like this version. However, I've developed my own definitions as they apply to making good career choices.

In 2009 our company established the goal of implementing a new software system for our manufacturing processes and customer order entry. We wanted this completed by the fourth quarter of 2010. A team of individuals worked diligently toward completing this goal for many months. We were confident we would reach this objective because the goal was in a SMART format and our team leader was measuring our progress as we completed the smaller goals. In November 2010 the new software system was successfully launched!

SMART goals work!

SMART Goal Example

Andrea's goal to be teaching English in Vietnam within a year was SMART. Making it into a future goal looks like the following:

Specific: She will teach English in Vietnam.

Measurable: To reach her goal, she will:
Step 1: Save money for the trip.
Step 2: Buy plane tickets.
Step 3: Complete necessary applications prior to going. These smaller steps help answer the question: How am I going to get there? She will measure her progress through the completion of the three smaller steps.

Attainable: Andrea knows she can teach English in Vietnam. Even more compelling is that others have gone before her.

Results-oriented: Her results are that she will be teaching in Vietnam and her students will be learning English.

Time-framed: within a year.

Just over a year later, in the fall of 2001, Andrea wrote me to say she would soon be leaving the United States to teach English in Vietnam. Andrea's example shows that creating a clearly defined goal in a SMART format works.

Sometimes other things result from SMART planning. Andrea met her future husband Alistair in Vietnam, and they were married in 2004.

Be sure that the goal you set for yourself is SMART. This can help paint a clear picture in your mind of what you will be working toward. The more you can visualize your objective, the greater chance you will have of completing it. Get started with defining a career goal for yourself by using the SMART Goals worksheet on the next two pages.

Worksheet Using SMART Goals

Where Am I?

Current situation: _____

_____

_____

_____

Where do I want to go? SMART Goal

Specific: _____

_____

_____

_____

_____

Measurable: _____

_____

_____

_____

Measure your progress by completing the smaller steps on the next page. These steps answer the question How am I going to get there?

From *Take Charge of Your Future: A 1-2-3 Guide to Making Good Career Choices* by Roderick S. Baker © 2013

*Step 1:*_____

_____

*Step 2:*_____

_____

*Step 3:*_____

_____

Attainable: _____

_____

_____

_____

Results-oriented: _____

_____

_____

_____

Time-framed: _____

_____

_____

_____

From *Take Charge of Your Future: A 1-2-3 Guide to Making Good Career Choices* by Roderick S. Baker © 2013

Avoid Fuzzy Goals

Don't set fuzzy goals. Two goal killers are:

> ➤ There is no completion date.
>
> ➤ There is no way to measure progress, or you simply don't measure your progress and stay on track.

For example: You have a goal to complete your fifteen-page political science paper a week before finals. One way to measure progress is by the number of pages you've completed each week. If you have completed ten pages by midterms, then you'll feel pretty confident you will complete your goal. If you wait to start until the night before your self-imposed goal, your chances of meeting your objective may be slim. You may still complete your goal, but the quality of your work may suffer. Give yourself the best chance to succeed by making intermediate steps and sticking to them!

Figuring Out Where You Want to Go

The answer to the question "Where do I want to go?" can be difficult to find. You may not know exactly where you want to go or what you want to do right now. That's OK. Talk with your teachers, your family, your friends, and people in the community. Each of these persons can mentor you on your journey. Read biographies of people who inspire you. Their stories can provide guidance.

You may want to "do it all." With so many career options to choose from, you may have a hard time deciding on a particular path. Working with a mentor and seeking guidance can help you decide on a path. Using the SMART format will enable you to make your dreams a reality. Answer the following questions on the next page to help you decide where you want to go.

Worksheet for Where I Want to Go

Where do I want to be in six months?

_____

_____

_____

Where do I want to be in one year?

_____

_____

_____

Where do I want to be in two years?

_____

_____

_____

Where do I want to be in five years?

_____

_____

_____

From _Take Charge of Your Future: A 1-2-3 Guide to Making Good Career Choices_ by Roderick S. Baker © 2013

When you consider your career, be sure to evaluate how you will support yourself. Will you make enough to pay off your student loans, support a family, or lead the kind of lifestyle that is important to you?

Once you have made a decision on where you want to go and put it into a SMART goal format, then you can ask yourself the third question...

Talk about journeys: the Great Wall of China is over five thousand miles long!

Step 3: How Am I Going to Get There?

A journey of a thousand miles begins with a single step.
—Lao-tzu, Chinese philosopher

How am I going to get there? Simply put: step-by-step. Each step completes a smaller goal toward your main objective. Practice in setting small goals and working toward them will help you in setting bigger goals—like making career choices. Your momentum builds as you move forward on your journey. Don't get discouraged by rocks in the path! Overcoming obstacles makes us stronger. In my own journey during my undergraduate years, I enjoyed studying language. I already had studied Spanish for two years in high school and was continuing to study it in college. One summer I decided I was going to take Japanese in addition to Spanish the coming fall. I had heard Japanese was difficult, so I studied the Japanese Hiragana all summer. When classes resumed in the fall, my first week of Japanese felt like we covered the entire summer's worth of material I'd been studying! I knew I was in for a big challenge. Seeking guidance from one of my political science professors, I explained the situation. I explained to him I wanted to learn Japanese in addition to Spanish. I thought both languages would help me on my path toward working in international relations. His simple advice was, "It's better to learn one language really well, than two languages only so-so. Pick your language." I decided to concentrate my efforts on Spanish and dropped the Japanese. While I was disappointed in not learning an important Asian language, I realized my professor was right. The emphasis I placed on learning Spanish helped me communicate with the local people when I became a Peace Corps Volunteer in Bolivia.

Sometimes the rocks you encounter in the road may cause you to make a choice between two very appealing options. You may have to give up something you wanted as I did in deciding to let go of Japanese while focusing on Spanish. Ultimately, I became much stronger in Spanish and was able to use that continuously for over two years in the Peace Corps, and frequently get to speak it today.

Live Each Day to the Fullest

Keep in mind what it means to live one day at a time.

> ➢ Don't worry about the future.
> ➢ Learn from the past.
> ➢ Live today as well as you can.

Most of the things we worry about never happen. Focus on what you have control over instead of the things you cannot control. That will help you reduce your worries and live a fuller life.

Let's go back to that evening in the Peace Corps when I was getting worked up about teaching agriculture in Spanish. As I sat in my room that night in Bolivia with my dinner in front of me, I realized that all I could do was eat dinner, finish my Spanish homework, and go to bed. Completing those things that night would help me on my way to becoming a Peace Corps Volunteer three months later. It would do me no good to worry about what had not yet happened. You still have to plan for the future, but don't lose sleep over it.

As you examine your SMART goal, continue to ask yourself: How am I going to get there? Keep your goal clearly in front of you. How are you measuring your progress? Check it frequently.

In the movie *Dead Poets Society*, the Latin phrase Carpe diem! (Seize the day!) is repeated by John Keating as played by Robin Williams. He inspires his students to do their best. As you strive to live each day to the fullest, make the best use of your time that you can. We all have the same number of hours, minutes, and seconds in each day. Dedicating time toward your goals on a daily basis will pay off!

Work hard! I've learned a lot from bestselling author Harvey Mackay over the years. He often quotes an old saying: "Perfect practice makes perfect."[3] When you work hard, be sure your technique is correct! You may have had a coach earlier in life or you may have one now who encourages you to master the fundamentals. Whether this is in athletics, the performing arts, or another activity, it is important to hone your technique before moving on to the next level. In the classes I have taught, I tell my students how important it is to write and keep practicing their writing. The majority of their assignments are writing papers. Clear and effective written communication is very necessary for nearly every job there is! In your classes ask your professors or teaching assistants to help you master the content of your coursework!

---

3   Check out http://www.harveymackay.com.

Learning, Change, & Networks

Continue to be a life-long learner in order to develop and refresh your skills. This will help you in making good career choices. Be flexible to change. In *Who Moved My Cheese?*, Spencer Johnson, MD, uses the story of two mice, Sniff and Scurry, and two "little people," Hem and Haw, to demonstrate what happens when our cheese (our job or something comfortable in our lives) is moved or goes away. Sniff and Scurry and Hem and Haw all live in a small world analogous to a 'maze'. In this world they depend on large mounds of cheese. Every day they go about their business. One day there is no more cheese! The two mice, Sniff and Scurry, quickly move on to find other cheese elsewhere. Hem and Haw, however, are in denial about their cheese being gone. Day after day they wait for the cheese to return. Finally, Haw decides nobody's going to bring the cheese back. He moves on and searches for cheese elsewhere. Ultimately, he finds new cheese and is very happy! Haw also learns how important it is to check on his cheese every day so he's prepared in case it gets moved elsewhere or is depleted. It's a great analogy to what can happen in our lives when something we were comfortable with every day completely changes. Change is inevitable. Continuing to learn and develop your skills will help you be prepared for change!

As you ask yourself how you are going to get there, work on developing a network. One of the best books you can read is *Dig Your Well Before You're Thirsty* by Mackay.[4] He offers great advice on how to develop a network, and how important it is to always deposit more into your network than you withdraw. What this means is to give more of yourself to others. People in your network will want to help you in your time of need if they see that you have always been there to help them.

You get more from giving to others than you do from receiving. Before I went into the Peace Corps, I had many former volunteers tell me that they felt they learned so much more from their experience than those they served learned from them. At the very least, you will feel great just by giving to others. As you develop your network and contribute to it, people in your network can help you with making good career choices.

As mentioned in Step 2, a mentor can help you on your career journey. Start looking for a mentor today within your network of people you know.

Choose your friends wisely. Betty M. Nelson, Purdue University dean of students emerita, says, "I think it is

---

4   Check out http://www.harveymackay.com/books.

enormously important to pick friends who will reinforce good qualities, high aspirations, integrity, [and] hard work."

As you network and talk with people, learn the steps that it takes to achieve your goal. My cousin Ivy wrote me while pursuing her PhD: "I've talked to several people over the years who decide to go to grad school or med school or have a certain career in mind and realize too late the number of prerequisites or other preliminary steps necessary to get to that stage. Or, if not too late, they find themselves going back and taking additional courses, delaying their eventual goals, because they didn't know the prerequisites existed."

Living on Your Own

How else are you going to reach your goal? For many, the time you spend in college is the first time you will be away from home. Keep these basic principles in mind:

➤ Get enough rest so you can stay awake in class and function properly (seven to eight hours of sleep per night).
➤ Develop the habit of being on time—this will serve you well in the work world, and your boss and co-workers will take note.

➢ Pay your bills on time—your credit rating depends on it.

➢ Exercise daily—this helps reduce stress.

➢ Eat nutritious food—you will look and feel better.

➢ Do your best—set your success bar based on what you can do without comparing yourself to others.

Save Money!

Don't forget about your finances.

➢ Make a budget.

➢ Don't spend more than you make.

➢ SAVE—have an emergency fund.

➢ Get a job if you need the extra cash.

While each of these can be a book in their own right, I'll briefly touch on each one here. Making a budget forces you to look at how much you are making and how much you are spending. Your only income at this point may come from student loans. When you make your budget, you itemize your income sources and all of your different spending categories: tuition, rent, food, gas, cell phone, money for 'fun', etc. Your budget clearly shows you how much you are bringing in and how much you are spending each month. There are many resources on the internet to help you create a budget. One resource is *Total Money Makeover* by Dave Ramsey.

Once you have your budget created, it's important to compare your income to your spending. If you are spending more than you are bringing in, you'll realize you won't be able to keep that up for very long. Or you may have to increase your student loans. It's okay to have student loans because you are investing in yourself. However, remember when you are standing in line for that double latte at your favorite coffee shop that you have to pay those loans back after graduation. You'll be paying interest on that double latte!

Financial experts often talk about having an emergency fund. The purpose of this is to have cash in the bank that you can access right away so you don't have to borrow on your credit card and pay high interest rates if you are unable to pay off your credit card balance. Experts often state an emergency fund of $1,000 is good to have, but this can be pretty steep while you are in college. Start with having an emergency fund of $300 or $500. This will come in handy if you have to make a small repair for your car. But keep this money for true emergencies and not for plane fare for spring break!

If your budget shows you are spending more than you are making or getting from student loans, then you might need to get a part-time job to help make up the difference. A job will not only help you create an emergency fund, but it will also provide some extra spending money.

Making a budget, not spending more than you make, and having an emergency fund will not only help you during college, these will also help you during career transitions.

Daily Reminders

Here are a few reminders as you start each day:

- ➢ Do it now!
- ➢ Handle papers only once—pick up an assignment and complete it.
- ➢ Review and assess your SMART goals.
- ➢ Work on the steps toward accomplishing your goals.
- ➢ Make a deposit into your network.
- ➢ Live each day to the fullest.
- ➢ Have fun!

Conclusion

As you embark on the next phase in your life's journey, follow the three steps below and reference the Quick Guide and Resources and worksheets. Good luck!

Step 1: Where Am I?

Take a personal inventory of yourself by writing in the worksheets or in a journal.

Step 2: Where Do I Want to Go?

Where do I want to be in six months? One year? Two years? Five years?

Set SMART Goals.

Step 3: How Am I Going to Get There?

➢ Making it step-by-step
➢ Living one day at a time
➢ Working hard
➢ Having fun

QUICK GUIDE & RESOURCES:

Step:	Main Points with Resources:
Where am I?	✓ Know Thyself; Be true to yourself ✓ Take the Myers-Briggs Type Indicator ✓ Establish your baseline **Resources:** ✓ Write in a journal (archival quality/acid free so the pages won't disintegrate over time)
Where do I want to go?	✓ Set SMART Goals: Specific, Measurable, Attainable, Results-oriented, and Time-framed **Read:** ✓ *Making Your Dreams Come True*—Marcia Wieder ✓ *The Lemming Conspiracy*—McDonald & Hutcheson
How am I going to get there?	✓ Step by Step, one day at a time, working hard & having fun—Read *The 7 Habits of Highly Successful People* by Stephen Covey

How am I going to get there? (continued)	✓ Carpe diem! Be a life-long learner and also flexible for change—Read *Who Moved My Cheese?* by Spencer Johnson, M.D. ✓ Develop a network and deposit more than you withdraw—Read *Dig Your Well Before You're Thirsty* by Harvey Mackay ✓ Finances: Budget, live within your means, save, have an emergency fund for career transitions—Read *Total Money Makeover Workbook* by Dave Ramsey

Worksheet for Self-Assessment

What do I like to do?

_____

_____

_____

What turns me off?

_____

_____

_____

What skills do I have?

_____

_____

_____

How do I share with others?

_____

_____

_____

How do I contribute to my family, school, and community?

_____

_____

_____

From _Take Charge of Your Future: A 1-2-3 Guide to Making Good Career Choices_ by Roderick S. Baker © 2013

Worksheet for Where I Want to Go

Where do I want to be in six months?

_____

_____

_____

Where do I want to be in one year?

_____

_____

_____

Where do I want to be in two years?

_____

_____

_____

Where do I want to be in five years?

_____

_____

_____

From *Take Charge of Your Future: A 1-2-3 Guide to Making Good Career Choices* by Roderick S. Baker © 2013

Worksheet Using SMART Goals

Where Am I?

Current situation: _____

_____

_____

_____

Where do I want to go? SMART Goal

Specific: _____

_____

_____

_____

_____

Measurable: _____

_____

_____

_____

Measure your progress by completing the smaller steps on the next page. These steps answer the question How am I going to get there?

From Take Charge of Your Future: A 1-2-3 Guide to Making Good Career Choices by Roderick S. Baker © 2013

Step 1:_____

_____

Step 2:_____

_____

Step 3:_____

_____

Attainable: _____

_____

_____

_____

Results-oriented: _____

_____

_____

_____

Time-framed: _____

_____

_____

_____

From *Take Charge of Your Future: A 1-2-3 Guide to Making Good Career Choices* by Roderick S. Baker © 2013

Peace Corps Volunteer Rodrigo with children of Ovejeros,
Bolivia, harvesting vegetables in the school garden.

Postscript

In late April 1994, our group of eighteen trainees was sworn in as United States Peace Corps Volunteers in Bolivia. We spread out in the country to do our part to fulfill the mission of the Peace Corps. An important part of that mission is to share our experiences with others once back in the United States. The twenty-seven months I was in Bolivia led to some of the most rewarding days of my life. My time there contributed to my perspectives on development, hands-on education, and sustainability both in international projects through Rotary as well as local projects in my work at RiverSide Electronics.

Just as the Peace Corps promotes serving others, the motto of Rotary International is "Service above Self."

To learn more, go to http://www.peacecorps.gov and http://www.rotary.org.

Index

About the Author

Author Roderick S. Baker is a former adjunct professor of global studies. He is a writer, speaker, and personal development mentor. A native of Flint, Michigan, he earned a BS in electrical engineering and a BA in political science from Purdue University in Indiana before serving for two years as a Peace Corps Volunteer in Bolivia. While in South America, Baker worked as a community-based agriculture volunteer. He later graduated from the Johns Hopkins School of Advanced International Studies in Washington, DC, with an MA in International Relations.

Baker has developed a unique philosophy that aims to help students in their career trajectory, and has incorporated aspects of these methods into his teaching at Winona State University. He is the Quality Manager for RiverSide Electronics, Ltd. and RiverBend Electronics, Ltd. in southeastern Minnesota. Baker works with university students as his company's co-operative education coordinator. Baker has served as the president of the Rotary Club of Winona, MN, and is a firm believer in the enduring virtues of community service.

http://www.takechargeseries.com

Made in the USA
Middletown, DE
04 January 2023

21405306R00033